When the clouds roll in

Finding contentment in the midst of the storm

By: Amy Maryon

Edited by: Corey Hostetter

When the clouds roll in: Finding contentment in the midst of the storm

Uncopyright 2015

Printed in the United States of America

This book is uncopyrighted. As with all my work, I operate on the honor system and pray that my readers do the same. If you do copy my information for the encouragement of others, please provide the source and ordering information. Thank you.

Scripture taken from the New King James Version (NKJV) of the Holy Bible, unless otherwise noted.

Published by Create space an Amazon company

For other books by this author visit: www.plainandnotsoplain.com

All the days of the desponding *and* afflicted are made evil [by anxious thoughts and forebodings], but he who has a glad heart has a continual feast [regardless of circumstances].

Proverbs 15:15 AMP

Dear Sister....

My prayer for this book is that you will be able to remove the storm clouds from your life. God wants you to have clear skies and fullness of Him. He doesn't want you to experience overcast or even partly cloudy days. He will remove all of the clouds and make your views of the heavens clearer than ever before. The only way that we can have fullness of life is by removing the hindrances that are clouding our relationship with God.

Who am I to be qualified to write on such topics? I am a woman just like you. I am a wife, a mom of ten children, and I have experienced the daily stresses of running a household by myself. I have gone through hardships, and experienced pain and disappointment. I went down the road of depression and bitterness, and it did nothing for me. When I started seeing the truths in God's word and really taking hold of what He promises, my life changed.

Our relationship with God is really meant to be life changing. You should see God manifest Himself in your life. You should be seeing Him work miracles in your life. It can happen, but you have to want Him to do that.

As with all relationships they take time. You can't just get close to God by going to church every week. You have to start spending time with Him each day. He needs to become part of your life. You also need to work on getting rid of things that are a hindrance to your relationship with Him.

The focus for this book will be on four hindrances, that I believe cloud out our vision of God and His wonderful power.

> Unforgiveness
> Taking offense
> Our need to control
> Devaluing ourselves

Be blessed as you strive to grow your relationship with the Lord.

Amy

How to use this book...

This book can be used for an individual looking to transform their relationship with God to a greater closeness. I would suggest reading through it and working on it as the Lord leads you. You may discover you need to stay on one area more than any others, and that is wonderful. That is seeing God work in your life. Prayerfully take the time to do the *"Action Steps"* to work out the things that need to be set free in your life.

It can also be used in a small group study. I would suggest breaking it up into four sessions. Take a topic each week and work on it. Read through the entire chapter together, stopping to reflect upon the different areas being discussed. Get into a time of quietness so each woman can listen to what the Lord is speaking to her. Pray through the prayers and have group members write down any areas God wants them to work on.

Throughout the week, they can continue applying the steps outlined in the book to work on the topic discussed. By the end of the week, they should have a testimony of what God is doing in their life.

Leaders be in contact during the week with each woman. As we know, when God starts moving in a person's life, Satan is right there to kill their joy. Encourage them, as they strive to overcome the hindrances in their life. Let them share what God has done at the next session.

When you are finished with the book, please send me a note to let me know how the Lord has worked in your life.

plainandnotsoplain@gmail.com

Be blessed as you desire more out of life!

Table of Contents

Storm clouds rolling in

It's 7:00 am, you awaken to the sound of a crying baby. One look at the alarm clock, makes you realize that you overslept, again. Time to jump out of bed, grab the baby, and sit down to feed her. If only she could eat faster, sigh. Your head is foggy from the lack of sleep last night. It seems the toddler wakes up more than the baby, and the preschooler is having a hard time sleeping through the night lately. You looked at the clock multiple times throughout the night and realize that you have been awoken every hour on the hour. You sigh and wonder if life will get any easier?

As you lay the baby back down, you decide to shower for a quick pick me up. It seems that this is the ONLY time that you are able to have a quiet moment with the Lord. It happens only as you are rinsing the shampoo out of your hair because you know that if you take more than the allotted seven minutes, your morning is going to be put further behind than it already is. You pray for patience, peace, and happiness for the day. You ask God to fill you because you are empty and feel so incomplete. Your mind starts to wander and you relive the things that your husband had said to you that stung your conscious last night. You start to think of your friend, whom you had lunch with yesterday, and how content and easy going she appeared while you visited. You listened to her share all that God was doing good in her life, and you outwardly rejoiced with her, but inside it hurt. Why wasn't He doing anything good in your life?

Now your mind starts racing. You begin to question yourself "Why can't I figure things out? I feel like such a failure as a wife and as a mom. I'm just not happy the way my life is going   Will I ever get through this?"

As the rest of your day unfolds, your mountain begins to grow. Between the crying babies, busy toddlers, and fighting preschoolers it seems that life is overwhelming. Your husband may call and ask you to take care of something unexpectedly and you get offended because of the bitterness you are still seething from last night. Doesn't he realize all that you are doing now? What he asks of you, you do it. But all the while you are thinking what a jerk he is for not realizing that you are busy enough.

As you continue to constantly dwell on all the negativity in your life, you feel like this cloud of doom is overtop of you. It is a heaviness that won't go away. The storm clouds continue to roll in day after day and cover you. Does it every go away? You pray and ask God for clarity and it seems He doesn't even answer. Inside you feel empty.

You go to church, searching for an answer to your problems. The pastor is preaching how important it is to get in the Word each and every day. In your head you are thinking there is absolutely no way that you can even think about having extra time for God. Can't God just listen and help fix things? You don't have time like these women that are so "spiritual" because you are focusing on raising your babies. But meanwhile you are drained. Everything you do, you wonder is any of it worth it? Church becomes a monotonous thing to attend. You just walk through the motions. You may experience "feelings" from the Holy Spirit, but as you leave, you forget what that was all about. You still continue living your days without the fullness of God. You are just being.

OVERCAST DAYS

Any of this sound familiar? For myself, this was reality. It seemed that life was overwhelming and I felt the cloud of doom rolling in, more times than I 'd like to admit. I tried to read my Bible and pray, but it just seemed that God wasn't listening to me. It took me awhile to get out of my misery. It took the prayers and help from some good faithful women who were willing to teach me and help me with my walk in the Lord. It seems I would get on track and do good for awhile and then something would happen and I would be back at the place I was before I had my "breakthrough." That isn't the way it should be. We should be having our breakthroughs and then continue moving forward . But it takes diligence and work. Yes, I said WORK.

Think of your relationship with your husband or children. If you only spent time together once a week, how is that relationship going to grow? It isn't. Relationships are going to take time, and lots of it. The more you are away and don't regularly share, the further you grow apart. You are more tempted to get your fellowship elsewhere and it is the same with God. If you aren't in regular commune with Him daily, you can't possibly get to know Him one on one.

TIME TO ROLL OUT THE CLOUDS

We have to know that we are full of God now. He lives inside of us and is able to do far more than we can ever imagine. We can' t look at our past or our circumstances and think we are lost. We have to know that God is so much greater than our problems in life.

Ephesians 3:20 says:

> *Now to Him who is able to do exceedingly abundantly above all that we ask or think, according to the power that works in us*

God's ability is far greater than anything that we can fathom. But, and yes there is always a but….. it is the **power** that works **within us** that determines that ability. That "power" is found in our soul.

We are made up of three parts: body, spirit, and soul. The body is our physical body, that holds everything into place. We then have our spirit, which when we accept Jesus, is made perfect. When we ask the Holy Spirit to dwell within us, that is what our spirit becomes. Our spirit will go on to live in eternity. We then have a soul. Our soul is our mind, will, and emotions. Our soul is what forms us to be the people that we are. It can get damaged and not work the way that it should based on life experiences, past hurts, and emotions. How do we fix our souls? By turning to the Word of God.

In Romans 12:2 it says:

And do not be conformed to this world, but be transformed by the renewing of your mind, that you may prove what is that good and acceptable and perfect will of God.

We are going to have to renew our minds from all that we have been taught in our lives. Everything that we go through in life leaves an impact on our souls. Some positive and some negative. How we react to people is based on what we have gone through. How we treat others and react to situations is based on what we have learned. Some of us have been damaged in our souls from traumatic experiences in childhood. It has hindered our walks in life. Many of us can trace back current problems with some instance that happened in our childhood. Isn't that crazy?? To think that our lives are controlled by that one negative instance! But because we came to know Christ, we don't need to be held to that bondage any longer. We can be set free from the wounds that we have encountered in our souls.

John 8:31-32

Then Jesus said to those Jews who believed Him, "If you abide in My word, you are My disciples indeed. And you shall know the truth, and the truth shall make you free."

You don't need to be trapped by Satan's snares any longer. You can be SET FREE! It all begins by making a decision to want to change your mind and heal your soul.

UNFORGIVENESS

Forgiveness is unlocking the door to set someone free and realizing you were the prisoner!"
— *Max Lucado*

Forgiveness, especially when given to others, is hard, but not impossible. For myself, being asked to let someone loose from the damage that they caused me was not something I was ready to hear. I didn't believe that person needed to be "set free" from my forgiveness. I wanted them to suffer for all the wrong that they had done to me. It is one of the hardest things to give away.

Forgiveness:

- to send forth, send away
- To remit or forgive debts or sins
- To let loose from

WHEN LIGHTNING STRIKES---MY TESTIMONY

When I was growing up, I was sexually molested by a family member. This was not someone in my own home, but it happened numerous times throughout my childhood. As a child, I didn't know what was going on, I just knew it was wrong. I lived with many conflicting thoughts as a child. Even as a young girl, I took other relationships that were probably very normal, but I twisted them in my own mind and made them out to be something that they were not. As I grew to be a teen, I used my sexual abuse as a crutch to what I was looking for in life. I did things that I am ashamed of, but I was a lost soul. I blamed most of my life on that predator for doing that to me. The ability to not forgive consumed me. It made me think dark, depressing thoughts. I reacted in anger, rebellion, self-centeredness, and depression.

Looking back, my mind was not my own. Satan definitely had a stronghold in my life and unknowingly I allowed him that authority.

I remember the night, I tried to take my own life. Satan was right there to help feed my mind with suicidal thoughts. I sat and listened to sad music that made me think of the things that I did not have. He gave me imaginary stories and thoughts about how others viewed me and what they thought of me. He let me know that I would not be missed, if I stepped out of this life. I was very good at listening to him and letting him control my life. I was almost letting him win.

I fell asleep hearing a thunderstorm in my mind. Then I heard a voice call out to me to get up. I ignored it. Several times throughout the night, the storm still raged, but that voice continued to call out to me. Even among my self-loathing, I remember hearing that "still small voice" and I know it was the voice of the Lord. He was trying to reach out to me one last time, but it was my choice whether or not I listened. I did.

I was treated poorly by most of the hospital staff, as just another, lost teen trying to get attention. It was hurtful. The shame and aloneness I was still feeling even after I didn't go through with Satan's plans, it seemed I couldn't get away from it. I didn't want to hold on. My mind wanted to give up. I wanted to end this misery.

Most of the nurses were gruff and angered and didn't want to deal with my mess. Then God sent someone. This older woman was very pleasant and kind to me. She smiled, held my hand, and prayed for me. She kept saying to hold on because God had a plan for my life and that I needed to pull through this. I didn't really think much about it at the time, but I remember the love she showed and it pulled me through.

It was still many years until I came to know the Lord after that moment. I continued to let the wounds in my soul fester and hurt. Bitterness had grown. I just kept trying to bandage it up the best I could. I smiled to cover up the pain, but I was still broken and empty on the inside. Most of my actions and responses in my life were rooted from that hurt. Even as a Christian, I blamed that person, for the troubles I was experiencing. Why wasn't I experiencing this "amazing" life that God had promised me?

I remember talking with a Christian woman about the bitterness I held onto, and she explained the need for forgiveness towards that family member who molested me. In my own mind, I was not into doing that. "How dare that person get forgiveness after they ruined my life! I was NOT going to let that person off the hook especially when they never even expressed any sort of responsibility for what they had done wrong". I attended church year after year. I prayed and it seemed I was never getting through to God. Wasn't I supposed to ask and I shall receive? Seems life was still a struggle and I wondered if being a Christian was really going to be any different.

Then I realized there had to be more to life than what I was doing. I started searching out scriptures with forgiveness.

> So My heavenly Father also will do to you if each of you, from his heart, does not forgive his brother his trespasses.

> Matthew 18:35

> For if you forgive men their trespasses, your heavenly Father will also forgive you.

> Matthew 6:14

> Judge not, and you shall not be judged. Condemn not, and you shall not be condemned. Forgive, and you will be forgiven

> Luke 6:37

MY MOMENT OF REVELATION

I needed to forgive so that God could forgive me! That was huge. I had to look at what Christ had done for me. Here was a man who did nothing wrong. He didn't deserve to die, but He was put to shame and death. He took all of the sins of mankind upon himself and died so that all of our sins could be forgiven. Even when he was on the cross, His words were to "forgive them Father, for they know not what they do." Those words echoed in my brain..........**"for they know not what they do."**

Seeing the Ray of Sunshine

People of the world do not know what they do. When someone isn't walking with the Lord as they should or even completely deny God any authority in their life, they are walking in darkness. When you walk in darkness you cannot see. You just do what "feels" good. You can compare it to the life of a bottom feeder fish. Those fish cannot see. They move around by pure feelings and emotions. Whatever feels good they do. If they want something they take it. They don't think about consequences or actions, they just do. The same is true for people. They walk around in blindness to what is going on.

For the hearts of this people have grown dull. Their ears are hard of hearing,
And their eyes they have closed

Acts 28:27

I had to look at my situation and realize that the people who hurt me were walking around in blindness. They took what they thought was theirs to take. They weren't thinking of eternity, they were just in darkness, moved by feelings.

If someone has hurt or wronged you, you need to forgive them. That person is walking in darkness. Even if they profess to be a Christian, you have to know that they are not walking in the light of Christ. They will be one of those people who *wreak iniquity, lawlessness,* and God will separate *them in the day of judgment* as stated in Matthew 7:23:

And then I will declare to them, 'I never knew you; depart from Me, you who practice lawlessness!'

WHAT DOES THE BIBLE SAY ABOUT FORGIVENESS?

One of the most well known teachings on unforgiveness is Jesus' parable of the unmerciful servant, which is recorded in Matthew 18:23-35...

Therefore the kingdom of heaven is like a certain king who wanted to settle accounts with his servants. And when he had begun to settle accounts, one was brought to him who owed him ten thousand talents. But as he was not able to pay, his master commanded that he be sold, with his wife and children and all that he had, and that payment be made. The servant therefore fell down before him, saying, 'Master, have patience with me, and I will pay you all.' Then the master of that servant was moved with compassion, released him, and forgave him the debt.

But that servant went out and found one of his fellow servants who owed him a hundred denarii; and he laid hands on him and took him by the throat, saying, "Pay me what you owe!' So his fellow servant fell down at his feet and begged him, saying, "Have patience with me, and I will pay you all." And he would not, but went and threw him into prison till he should pay the debt. So when his fellow servants saw what had been done, they were very grieved, and came and told their master all that had been done. Then his master, after he had called him, said to him, "You wicked servant! I forgave you all that debt because you begged me. Should you not also have had compassion on your fellow servant, just as I had pity on you?' And his master was angry, and delivered him to the torturers until he should pay all that was due to him.

"So My heavenly Father also will do to you if each of you, from his heart, does not forgive his brother his trespasses."

In this parable, a king forgives a servant an enormously large debt. Later, that same servant refuses to forgive the small debt of another man. The king hears about this and rescinds his prior forgiveness. Jesus concludes by saying, *"This is how my heavenly Father will treat each of you unless you forgive others from your heart."*

Don't be confused and think that God's forgiveness is based on our works and what we do. Forgiveness and salvation are founded completely in the person of God and by Jesus' redeeming work on the cross. The Bible says in Ephesians 2:8: *For by grace you have been saved through faith, and that not of yourselves; it is the gift of God, not of works, lest anyone should boast.* However our actions demonstrate our faith and the extent to which we understand God's grace that has been given to us.

When we truly grasp the greatness of God's gift to us, we can easily pass this gift along to others. We have been given grace and should return grace to others. When reading this parable it seems appalling for the servant to not forgive the debt especially after he was forgiven of such a large debt. But when we are unforgiving in our own hearts, we act just as the servant in the parable did.

THE AFTERMATH: CONSEQUENCES OF UNFORGIVENESS:

Choosing not to forgive can cause five things to happen in your life:

- Emotional problems
- Increase in bitterness
- Physical ailments
- Gradual withdrawal from spiritual things
- Allows Satan a stronghold in your life.

Emotional problems

The results of unforgiveness to others will lead to emotional problems in our own lives. Even the secular world would agree on the importance of forgiving others. When you allow the other person to "win" with what they have done to you, it puts you in an emotional ditch. When problems and life occur, it is so much easier to keep throwing all of the problems on top of what you are already dealing with and cause yourself to fall into further depression.

Bulimia can have its roots with unforgiveness and bitterness from the past. It could be critical words from a parent or a close friend that caused hurt. If not forgiven it only ends in mental bondage and can lead to more emotional problems.

Being a woman who suffered abuse as a child and choosing not to forgive can also add to emotional problems in life. She may feel beaten down and never "good enough' for anyone. Her sense of worth is low and she continues to return to relationships that are not healthy for her. She allows the cycle of abuse to continue in her life and into the lives of her children. "I deserve this," she makes herself believe. She misses out on the goodness that God has for her because she can't let go of unforgiveness in her past.

We have talked about forgiving others, but what about forgiving ourselves? Have you made wrong decisions in your own life that you need to forgive yourself of? It could be forgiving yourself of a past decision of abortion. How about any sins that you may have committed in secret? Do you do things that you are shameful of ? Things you think no one else knows about? We know that God knows all and can see us even when we are in secret. Even though you know that God can forgive you of your sins and wipe out all your transgressions, can you forgive yourself of what you have done? When we don't allow ourselves to be forgiven, we are holding onto the emotional baggage and it is going to hold us back from God.

Increase in bitterness

Unforgiveness also leads to bitterness. We view others and circumstances in anger and then it causes bitterness to take root. It robs us of the full life that God intends for us to have.

Make every effort to live in peace with everyone and to be holy; without holiness no one will see the Lord. See to it that no one falls short of the grace of God and that no bitter root grows up to cause trouble and defile many.

Hebrew 12:14-15

Even though we may not think people deserve forgiveness, we need to give it. By God's standards, we don't deserve His forgiveness either, but He gives it. We need to demonstrate the same love that God shows to us. If we don't show others what the love of God can do, who is going to show them? How is our world going to change if no one is willing to do that? We know in whom we live and whom our joy is found. Others do not know or understand that kind of love and they walk in darkness.

Remember that when we forgive others, it frees us from the *sin of unforgiveness*. The ones we don't want to forgive, who did wrong to us, are going to be held accountable by God. When we choose to forgive, we release that person from his liability to us. We relinquish the right to seek personal revenge and to not hold his wrongdoing against him. However, we do not necessarily allow that person back into our circle of trust or even release that person from the consequences of their sin. In Romans 6:23 it states that the *wages of sin is death*. We know that God's forgiveness relieves us from eternal death, but it does not release us from consequences of sin. (e.g., speaking of the justice system) We also don't have to act as though nothing has been done wrong. It only means that we recognize that grace is abundant, has been given to us, and that we have no right to hold someone else's sins over their head.

Physical ailments

When we choose to not forgive someone it can also affect us physically. Many women struggle with weight issues, sleep issues, high blood pressure, anxiety, and a multitude of other health issues that have roots embedded in unforgiveness and bitterness. Why are you going to allow another person's sin to ruin your life physically? You cannot. It is not worth letting them ruin it. You deserve so much more.

Gradual withdrawal from spiritual things

When we choose to not forgive, it puts a hinder on our prayers to the Lord.

And whenever you stand praying, if you have anything against anyone, forgive him, that your Father in heaven may also forgive you your trespasses. But if you do not forgive, neither will your Father in heaven forgive your trespasses."

Mark 11:25-26

The Bible says that if we don't forgive others, then He won't forgive us. When we continue to pray and ask God for things it may seem that He never answers our prayers, and we wonder why. Meanwhile we have this unforgivness in our hearts that we are not giving over to the Lord. Our spiritual growth comes to a stop. Things don't seem to work out. We lose our joy and our happiness. Gradually we become less and less interested in the things of God because we aren't seeing things bear fruit in our lives. How can we ask God for anything when we can't do the most basic thing that God does for us?

Allows Satan to build a stronghold in your life

If you are allowing Satan to be part of your life, he won't stop at just being a "part," he wants all of it. He will continue to peck away at the other areas of your life until they are completely taken over by him. But it doesn't have to be this way. God is bigger than Satan but we MUST give him first place in our lives. We cannot allow any door to be left open to allow the enemy to come and steal away the goodness that you have found in God.

TAKE ACTION: STEPS TO HEALING UNFORGIVENESS

1. Recognize and forgive
2. Heal your wounds
3. Speak words of God's promise

Step One: Recognize and forgive

Now that we know the importance of forgiving others, we need to take action and do it. It begins with prayer. You need to sit quiet with the Lord. Ask God to clear your mind and to fill you with the Holy Spirit. Then ask him to bring to mind anyone or anything that you need to forgive. Be quiet and let the work of the Holy Spirit take place. Sometimes we keep talking and don't allow God to answer. Keep focusing on God during this time. When he brings the person or thing to mind, thank Him and take hold of it and say, "I release this person in the name of Jesus to you Lord and I forgive them of the wrongs that they have done to me. I give them to you and let your will be done with them." Move away from the role of victim and release the control and power that the offending person and situation has had in your life.

**There may be multiple people or situations in your life that you need to forgive, I would suggest working through them one at a time to complete the healing process.

Step two: Heal your wound

What happens next is dealing with your soul wound. Your spirit has been wounded from what has happened to you. In the Bible it is known as a broken or crushed spirit.

A man's spirit sustains him in sickness, but a crushed spirit who can bear?

Proverbs 18:14

A cheerful heart is good medicine, but a crushed spirit dries up the bones

Proverbs 17:22

He restores my soul; He leads me in the paths of righteousness For His name's sake

Psalm 23:3

Most of our soul wounds are deeply rooted within us. We may have lived for so long in this wounded state that we just come to accept that life is just this way. Maybe it is causing a physical ailment or some emotional problem, whatever the case, you need to heal your soul wounds so that you can move forward in your life. Many of our current problems are deeply rooted and traced back to traumatic and hurtful instances in our past. These are wounds in our soul. Once you release that wounding event or that person who wronged you, you can finally begin to heal your brokenness in your body.

Much more then, having now been justified by His blood, we shall be saved from wrath through Him.

Romans 5:9

In Him we have redemption through His blood, the forgiveness of sins, according to the riches of His grace

Ephesians 1:7

How much more shall the blood of Christ, who through the eternal Spirit offered Himself without spot to God, cleanse your conscience from dead works to serve the living God?

Hebrews 9:14

The blood of Jesus is what wipes everything clean. We ourselves can try and bandage up our wounds. But over time, the bandage will only become loose and fall off. You will return to old sinful ways and your problems will become a continuous cycle. You will wonder why you can't get out of this lifestyle. You need to wipe it clean.

Sit quietly with the Lord, ask Him to take that wound and fill it with the blood of Jesus. Let the healing power of the blood encompass it completely. Do not leave any room for the devil to get in. Just sit quietly and let the Holy Spirit do the work. Think about that wound being healed entirely, back to its perfect state. When you feel at peace, thank the Lord for His healing.

Step three: Speak words of God's promise

How do we overcome things in this world?

We overcome by the blood of the Lamb and the word of our testimony.

Revelation 12:11

...to call things that are not as though they were

Romans 4:17

We need to continually speak praise about our healing and don't let the doubt back in. Even when your mind starts to replay the events, immediately speak the Word of God to confess your healing.

Be Ready!

What happens when you are going to have a spiritual breakthrough? The Bible says in Luke 8:12 that *immediately the devil comes and takes away the Word from their hearts, so that they may not believe and be saved.* Satan knows exactly when something good is going to happen, because he comes immediately to try and thwart your progress with negativity.

When Jesus was in the desert for forty days, the one who came to try and make him doubt was Satan. He will immediately come when you are going to have a breakthrough to make you doubt what you are doing. When you hear that voice, tell it to go away in the name of Jesus, you don't need to listen to it.

Be consistent in speaking healing and positiveness in your life, and Satan will learn to know that he can't get to you anymore. Your wound will be healed by the words you speak.

THE BENEFIT OF GOD'S WORD

Continue to speak healing, peace, and joy in your life. Look up Bible verses that pertain to your situation and what God has healed you from. I would suggest that you copy them and put them in areas where you can constantly be reminded of what the Lord has done.

He heals the brokenhearted, and binds up their wounds.

Psalm 147:3

Be anxious for nothing, but in everything by prayer and supplication, with thanksgiving, let your requests be made known to God; and the peace of God, which surpasses all understanding, will guard your hearts and minds through Christ Jesus.

Philippians 4:6-7

For God has not given us a spirit of fear, but of power and of love and of a sound mind

2Timothy 1:7

Declare over your life...

I am a child of a loving God. I am made in the image and likeness of God and He has made me perfect in every way. He has given me peace, power, love, and forgiveness, He has a perfect plan for my life and He wants me to move forward with that plan. I am free from unforgiveness and can come humbly before the Lord with my requests. No matter what has happened in my past, it has been washed away and a new creation has been made. This creation is going to go out boldly into the world and proclaim the goodness of the Lord and do His will. I have been healed from unforgiveness, my soul has been restored. I am left with peace that passes understanding and that gives me unspeakable joy. My life is good because of Jesus Christ.

Progress continues...

To ensure progress with success, you will need to repeat these steps. Continue until you feel that you have no more unforgiveness causing bad roots in your life.

Then they cry out to the LORD in their trouble,
And He brings them out of their distresses.
He calms the storm,
So that its waves are still.
Then they are glad because they are quiet;
So He guides them to their desired haven
Psalm 107:28-30

God wants to bless you and help you overcome in your life. But we have to cry out to Him. He won't force us. We need to want to change and become even greater. Once we do that, we will have real gladness in our hearts.

Use the next few pages, to write what the Lord is speaking to you about the need of unforgivness in your life. Sit quietly with Him throughout the week and write what He speaks to your mind. This is a good visual reminder of God working in your life. Then apply the steps outlined in this chapter and have faith that God has removed the wound from your life. When you are truly freed from it, you will be able to come back and read through your notes and notice it will not have any effect on you. Then you will know you have been set free!

BEING OFFENDED

An offending heart is the breeding ground for deception

John Brevere

Many of us have "pet peeves" or things that offend us in life. We can get offended in grocery stores by the cashier taking too long, while driving in traffic behind a slow moving vehicle, by our Pastor speaking something we don't want to hear, by friends saying things that are usually taken the wrong way, and we can get offended by God because He didn't answer our prayer the "right way." Maybe our life isn't going a certain way so we get mad. This in turn, goes hand in hand with how we react and respond in life.

We get offended so we stop doing something. We may stop giving to church, we may stop attending church or a group, we may even stop praying. We sit and hurt and seethe. All this does nothing but hurt us. We may "think" we are punishing the other person, but we are only hurting ourselves. Life around us still goes on, just with us not in it. Now we are alone. Alone with our thoughts of self-pity and hurt. We sit and think things through more than we should. Satan has set the trap and has us caught!

Offense:
- To set a snare
- to put a stumbling block in the way

WHEN STORMS SURGE...MY TESTIMONY

That was me. I went through life and thought it wasn't fair that I had to do what I did when no one else seemed to have the problems that I faced. There were many times when I was angered at God and other people for my "lot" in life. But you know, none of that mattered. None of it hurt anyone but ME. I was the one that suffered with anger and built up frustration. It only led to me taking offense the next time I ran into someone and they said something that "rubbed me the wrong way."

Offenses didn't just begin. They came slowly. It started with something that someone would say that hurt me, but I suppressed the feelings and went on with life. Then something else would happen and I would start to burn inside. More events would happen over the course of days or weeks and this little pile of offenses would keep building and building until something little would ignite it and some unfortunate person would get the brunt of it. Most of the time it was my husband and children. Afterwards, I would feel guilty. I would pray and ask God to help me rid myself of my anger, but it seemed it wasn't going away. Every time I would get offended that fire rekindled and burned deep inside of me and then it would explode into a rage at something so small. It made no sense to me that I was not able to control it. What was I doing wrong?

WHAT DOES THE BIBLE SAY ABOUT OFFENSES?

We can't go to God and have Him fix things if we don't know what the Word of God says. God wants us to FIRST get rid of our offense so that we can worship and come to Him freely. The Bible says in Matthew 5:24 that we are to *leave our gifts at the altar, go and be reconciled to our brothers FIRST, and then come back and offer our gifts.* When we do this, He can accept our worship, listen to our prayers, and answer them.

But what if you say that you don't actually "hate" someone you are just offended by them? You may be right. Offenses by themselves are generally not anger, hurt feelings, or resentment. But those annoyances and irritations have the unfortunate ability to build into grudges. These usually lead to sins that a person has allowed themselves to be led into. The sad part is that it is usually done by the persons own mind. After some time your heart can become hardened and anger takes root. You may not think of it as anger but that is what it is called. They build upon each other little by little until your love has grown cold towards them. It causes our hearts to shut out the goodness and blessing that God has for us.

And then shall many be offended, and shall betray one another, and shall hate one another.

Matthew 24:10

If we truly want to be free and live life to the fullest, then we need to stop taking offense.

BEING A WATCHMAN FOR OFFENSES IN OUR LIVES

There are four ways in which you can be offended in your life:

1. Offended by the truth
2. Offended by circumstances
3. Offended by ourselves
4. Offending others

Let's examine these in depth, so that we can be aware of when we are beginning to get offended at things.

Offense #1 The truth

And you shall know the truth, and the truth shall make you free.

John 8:32

When we hear the truth, for the most part, we would assume it is good. But when we are prideful and hear something that goes against what we have been taught or brought up with it can be hard to accept. Obeying and accepting what is true from God can reap many good things, unlike the world's truth. When we hear the truth and act upon it, it sets our present conditions into line with God and it prepares us for far greater blessings than we can imagine. We want to be moving forward in our walk with the Lord. We don't want to stay stagnant. How much better is a life that is lived to the fullest just by laying aside our pride and becoming meek and submissive to what God has for us?

For many, they make excuses of why they don't want to change or don't want to hear certain truths. All those excuses are doing nothing but preventing them from moving forward. We want to be FREE!!! We want to be free so that God can use us in a mighty way.

I remember very much when God's word—the truth---was teaching me how to change things about myself. I thought in my own mind that I was a pretty good person, but I realized I had a lot of hidden attitudes and heart issues to work on. There was more than one time that I felt like I didn't want to do this. God was showing me how I had prideful, control issues. I wanted to take charge and fix things. I wanted to do things my way, because I thought it was best. He was showing me that I was a manipulator, and that I had to stop feeling sorry for myself. I had to let down my guard and humble myself before my family and God. It was tough. But I kept on it. It was stretching me and it was not comfortable. But just as a caterpillar stretches out of a cocoon and transforms into a butterfly, that is the same metamorphosis that we go through. When we are stretched, it may feel a little uncomfortable but that is where we are able to push through and enter into the next level of what God has for us.

Offense #2 Circumstances of life

The parable of the sower:

The sower sows the word. And these are the ones by the wayside where the word is sown. When they hear, Satan comes immediately and takes away the word that was sown in their hearts. These likewise are the ones sown on stony ground who, when they hear the word, immediately receive it with gladness; and they have no root in themselves, and so endure only for a time. Afterward, when tribulation or persecution arises for the word's sake, immediately they stumble.

Mark 4:14-17

This truth is an important one, you see it happening every day. If someone is not deeply rooted in God's word, when trouble comes, they fall away. This is a big testimony that I know I have encountered many times throughout my life. People appear to have such a deep personal relationship with the Lord, but then hard times fall. Instead of digging deep into God's word and turning to Him for strength and guidance, they crumble and fade away. It is a sad reality. God's word tells us about it so that we can be aware and careful not to do it.

When we are faced with trials or bad situations they can either make us stronger or they will make us resentful. When bad things happen, if we take offense at the situation, we start to blame others for it. We may blame God for disrupting our cushy lifestyles. We may even blame the devil---and that is rightly so. But we can also take offense at other people who seem to be more blessed than we are. Sometimes it is just resentment. That resentment takes root to form bitterness towards life and the situations that come our way. But we must be made aware of resentment. This is part of not taking offense.

When we are faced with these trials or bad situations we need to look at them from a whole new perspective. We need to think, that by going through this, it can actually help us get deeper and stronger roots in our relationship with God.

Personally, when I was alone and went through trials, I had only one person to hang onto, and that was God. During those times is when my faith was strengthened. I realized that once I gave over my situations to Him, He could do far greater of a job than I could ever do. Seeing His hand do the things that for years I tried to control and change was pretty amazing.

When times of trial arise you can really see how faithful you truly are to God. Emotional hearers of the Word always fall apart during times of trial. They become unstable. They get angry and make accusations against others, instead of rationally looking at the situation. This is only a sign of spiritual immaturity. Not that you can't get emotional during times of trial---but what I am saying is that inside, your faith will help you stand the test of your trials. Knowing that God is in control and that He will work ALL things out together for your good. Be careful to guard, and to not let your emotions take charge of your faith.

When bad things or situations happen in your life, don't blame God. Lamentations 3:25-28 says that God *lays the yoke of divine discipline on us for our benefits*. Sometimes it is good for us to experience disappointment. We learn to just shake off the dirt, get back up, and go on. We learn not to place our hope in things, but to place our hope in God. When we don't get our way all of the time, we learn to appreciate things much more. We grow very thankful for the things that we do have. God is at work ALL OF THE TIME. We must trust God and NEVER accuse Him of not caring.

Offense #3 Offended by ourselves

If your hand or foot causes you to sin, cut it off and cast it from you. It is better for you to enter into life lame or maimed, rather than having two hands or two feet, to be cast into the everlasting fire. And if your eye causes you to sin, pluck it out and cast it from you. It is better for you to enter into life with one eye, rather than having two eyes, to be cast into hell fire.

Matthew 18:8-9

In these verses God is referring to "cutting out" and getting rid of the things that are causing you to stumble in your life. Having a guilty conscience is a major problem in life. It causes you to shrink back in fear of people finding out your "hidden" sin. You will lack boldness to stand for things God wants you to stand for. When Jesus died on the cross He did it to set us free from condemnation and feelings of guilt. But it is our choice to make right decisions once we accept that He did that for us. We cannot continue to choose sinful behaviors and expect to receive the blessings and benefits of knowing Jesus. His blood bought our freedom. But if we remain in sin when we know that it is wrong, then we are not using the freedom He gave us.

How can we go about not offending ourselves? First we accept and call it what it is, SIN. Stop excusing away your problems. State it, name it, then avoid it!! Stop participating in that which is causing you to sin.

There are so many different things that are stumbling blocks in our lives. We need to cut them out and throw them away.

This can include some of the following:

- Magazines with immodestly dressed people.
- Movies that you would NOT sit with Jesus and watch.
- Dirty jokes, bad language, gossip with people.
- Music that does not have a positive message.
- Books that cause you to dream up images of sinful things.
- Friends that lead us to do things that are not godly.

Offense #4 Giving offense to others

We give no offense in anything, that our ministry may not be blamed

2 Corinthians 6:3

A brother offended is harder to win than a strong city,
And contentions are like the bars of a castle

Proverbs 18:19

I like both of these verses. Not being an offensive person is a HUGE way to share the testimony of Christ in your life. If we as Christians walk around with sinful behaviors, attitudes, and lifestyles how is anyone else, whom has those same issues going to want to change things in their own life? Why would they want a "God" who doesn't even manifest himself in them? One who doesn't help them change from their wrong ways? People are looking for a way out. They want to get away from their worldly lifestyles and ways. If we can't show it to them, and prove how much better our lives are, then why would they want what we say God offers?

What is the best way to avoid giving offense to other people?

Think before you do or say something!!!

If we were just to "think" a moment before we start to speak, we can usually avoid offending someone. The Bible says it is hard to tame the tongue. For many of us, we just speak before we think. When our friends are sick with the flu for weeks on end and we start talking about how we prayed and did not get that sickness---we are causing offense to someone. When we go minister in a low income area and we choose to wear expensive clothing or jewelry, we are probably going to cause some offense. If we know people are struggling with sin in their lives and we prance around dabbling in the sin—because we don't have issues with it, we are causing offense. For example, if we have a glass of wine at dinner in front of a friend who is struggling with alcoholism.

If you are in a disagreement with someone, the best thing you can do is stay calm. Allow others to have their way in the conflict. By choosing to remain calm and not be part of the disagreement puts a quick end to the anger and will stop the offense. Being a part of foolish and dumb arguments is NOT a sign of a believer. God wants us to be the peacemakers, helping others to learn to have self control in their lives.

Be considerate of others and think how they feel in their own situation. The saying "put yourself in someone else's shoes" is a huge reminder of how we are to walk around in love and not in offense.

THE IMPACT OF TAKING OFFENSE

When we go about our life and someone or something comes our way that "hits a nerve," we react negatively and then BAM, we are offended! It happens suddenly, it doesn't usually take time to sink in, we are either easily offended or not. It is like a wound that refuses to get better. It festers, continues to open, reddens, and gets infected. It hurts and keeps infecting our life with anger, bitterness, un-forgiveness, sickness, and strife. It will rob us of so many good things that God has for us. When we react like this it is a good indicator that we have a wound. Whenever we find ourselves responding like this we need to be asking the Holy Spirit to reveal what needs to be dealt with.

For most people, it is hard to forgive. They might get to the point of forgiveness but they don't usually forget. Satan knows if we don't forgive then he can bring that offense up over and over again. He will use it as a tool against us to keep opening that wound and dig deeper, to cause bitterness in our soul. He LOVES to see us miserable and so loathed in our own self pity.

For we do not wrestle against flesh and blood, but against the rulers, against the authorities, against the cosmic powers over this present darkness, against the spiritual forces of evil in the heavenly places.

Ephesians 6:12

We have to remember that we are not striving against people, but against demonic forces that are trying to oppress us. When we allow ourselves to get offended it is like stepping into that trap. Remember the definition from the beginning? Offense is a snare set by Satan. We cannot get out until we forgive and release the other person from the offense.

Holding onto bitterness and anger only causes us to be affected physically, emotionally, and spiritually.

Physically it will create stress in the body, as the body no longer can function doing the natural processes of day to day. It has to work hard to help ward off the excess pumping of the heart due to stress and anger. This causes a weakness in the body, which in turn can lead to sickness, tiredness, and more stress on your heart. Repeated anger over the years leads to a multitude of health problems, as in high blood pressure and heart conditions. How easy it sounds to take care of our bodies physically by not taking offense at things?

Emotionally is a big one. How many of you deal with depression and sadness in your life? I know I did for years even after I was a believer. I would let offenses eat at me for days on end. I let Satan beat me down and make me believe I was not worth something. DO NOT let Satan work on you through offenses and make you believe you are not someone highly favored by the Lord. Our minds are a delicate thing. When offense comes your way DON'T TAKE IT!

Spiritually, offenses will not allow us to move to that next level that God has for us. We all should work towards a greater goal in life. We want to strive to keep working towards learning and experiencing a greater level of spiritual-ness that can only come from God. Most people never get to experience this awesomeness from the Lord. They are stuck in bondage of sin and it happens because of them choosing to take offense at things.

The less offense we take the happier we will become and the more peace we will have in our lives. When our hearts are free and there is no offense then we can just love other people. When you are free to love people without offense that is the biggest thing in life. Jesus calls us to love others in this way. We will get the most reward by taking this approach.

I pray that your love will overflow more and more, and that you will keep on growing in knowledge and understanding. For I want you to understand what really matters, so that you may live pure and blameless lives until the day of Christ's return.

1 Philippians 9-10

Paul prays this so that love would abound more and more in our hearts. We will have love in our hearts and will not take offense or give offense to others because the first thing that flows out of our lives is love. Let love at all times keep you in a place where you can just love others. The more that you can get your mind off of yourself, the happier you will be.

We may think it is hard to live this life as a Christian, but it is nothing compared to the life of a sinner. It is hard work to be a sinner and live a life of hopelessness. Having no one or way to turn to in life and just going about in our own sinful desires is hard. People of the world when in times of need or desperation have nowhere to turn. They give into Satan and let him destroy them. They may "think" that they need no God to help them in life, but trials and tribulations WILL COME. *Woe to the man who does not put his trust in God almighty.*

Another reason of why we should not take offense is because it is NOT always about "ME!!". Some think that everything in life is about "them." When someone is angry and retaliates against us, we take it personally. The majority of the time, it is about that other person and their own issues they are working out. We have to stop living irrationally or self-absorbed in our lives. This causes much needless suffering. When someone says something mean and condescending it is usually due to their own insecurities in life and they are speaking them out in hopes of sounding better themselves. We have to be on guard and be smarter than they are. A person being inconsiderate about missing an important date or being spiteful in some remark is a direct reflect of a fault in them not you. This fault in the other person does not need to become part of your problems ---so don't allow it!

Take Action: Steps to overcoming Offense

1. When to deal with it

2. How to deal with it

3. Why to deal with it

Step one: When to deal with it

The best time to deal with offense is the moment it happens.

> *Stay alert! Watch out for your great enemy, the devil. He prowls around like a roaring lion, looking for someone to devour.*
>
> *1 Peter 5:8*

We need to RESIST the devil at his onset. He is looking for a door to enter into your life. DO NOT let him get into your mind. If someone has offended you or something has happened between you and another, do as it says in Matthew 18:15:

> *If another believer sins against you, go privately and point out the offense. If the other person listens and confesses it, you have won that person back*

It says to privately win back your brother, you are to follow this pattern. If you continue reading to the next verse it states that you are to do this first and if they do not listen, take two or three people with you to talk with them. How many times do we just skip this part of the verse and go to someone else for "advice?" Don't go with an attitude of anger or righteousness. Go and say, "*I am sorry the devil is messing with me on this so I* need to say something"......or you can say..."*Maybe you meant nothing by this, but I felt offended because...."*

Usually others don't think about what they say and they don't intend of it sounding the way you took it. You can avoid all kinds of trouble by following the principles God has laid out for us. We can create heaps of offense by going to the wrong people---go to the one that offended and state your case peacefully.

Most important of all, continue to show deep love for each other, for love covers a multitude of sins.

And above all things have fervent love for one another, for "love will cover a multitude of sins.

1 Peter 4:8

This is all about growing our relationship with God and experiencing freedom in Christ. We should want every blessing that God has for us. We need more and more of His grace so that we can handle situations with people in a godly way, not in a carnal way. Can you imagine someone saying...*"I am so grateful that you brought that up because I did not even know I was doing that."* How much better could a situation go if we approached things this way?

God sent his Son so that we can live a life full of His love. We want to abound with his greatness. I love a word that will propel me to a higher level. Love covers a multitude of sins.

Offense will keep us from loving people. When we have unforgiveness and don't deal with the little stuff, it grows. It is not our job to take offense. It is our job from God to act without defense. Jesus did not take offense. He was a man who was rejected, abused, and He even had his friends go to sleep on Him when he asked them to pray. Why didn't he take offense? Because he knew WHERE HE CAME FROM AND WHERE HE WAS GOING! If anyone can know that, then they can have complete peace in their lives.

Your value is NOT determined by how someone has treated you. KNOW WHO YOU ARE!!

Step two: How to deal

How do we deal with offenses? We go to the Word of God. In 1 Samuel 16 , you can read the story of David. I will paraphrase it here. God told Samuel to go down to Jesse and choose a boy among his sons whom He has chosen to be the next king of Israel. All of the brothers were ready to be chosen, but Samuel did not choose any of them. When he asked if there were any others, David's dad responded with "Well, yeah there is David out in the fields." This is a prime example of someone not taking offense. Think if your dad had all of your brothers lined up ready to be chosen to be king and he did not even bother to get you. I would think that if you wanted a good time to take offense that would be one of those times. But David did not complain, and what did God do? He had the prophet choose David right in front of his brothers. Can you imagine, all of David's brothers lined up waiting to be chosen and here comes along the most unlikely candidate? I am sure his brothers were complaining and seething!

As we continue on with the story of David, we come to where he is to fight Goliath. He doesn't get why any of these soldiers did not want to fight Goliath. The reason David wanted to fight is because he knew God would fight with him. Why was he so sure that God would be with him? Because he KNEW God. David spent his days alone tending the sheep. This enabled him much quiet time with the Lord. When you get lonely, don't ever get mad at God, take it and use it as a time with Him.

The quieter you become, the better you can hear God.

More and more as we read David's story we see how his brothers tried to diminish him. They didn't want him to think that he had any value and so they condescended him. They were angered and jealous within themselves so they took their frustration out on him. But he was used to it and so he responded by turning away. He knew not to take offense.

David was out tending the sheep in the field. It does not sound like much of a noble job, but he was doing what he was supposed to be doing. God came and plucked him out from his place, to be positioned as king! When you are doing what you are supposed to be doing and having that close relationship with the Lord, you never know when God will choose you to do something greater.

Don't let anyone diminish what you do or make you feel belittled. Any job that God has given you to do, is a job that is important. If you are "just" a stay at home mom, thank the Lord that you are willing to raise up mighty warriors for Him. If you "just" clean houses, thank God for being a person willing to be a servant for another. God cares ONLY about the part He has asked you to do. We all have roles and purposes to fulfill here on this earth, we do them to the best of our ability and wait for the blessings to flow.

Step three: Why to deal with it

All of this centers around how this anger affects our prayers. If you are going to pray for something, you should be praying because you want them to get answered.

> Then Jesus said to the disciples, "Have faith in God. I tell you the truth, you can say to this mountain, May you be lifted up and thrown into the sea, and it will happen. But you must really believe it will happen and have no doubt in your heart. I tell you, you can pray for anything, and if you believe that you've received it, it will be yours. But when you are praying, first forgive anyone you are holding a grudge against, so that your Father in heaven will forgive your sins, too.
>
> Mark 11:22-25

If you are going to complain about something, don't bother to pray about it. God doesn't answer complaints, he answers prayers. God says that whenever you stand praying, if you have anything against anyone, first forgive before you pray. This includes any offenses against your neighbor, your husband, the lady at the store, a friend, etc. Any type of offense no matter how big or small WILL hinder your ability to have prayer answered.

Seeing results that work!

Taking offense is a high price to pay for something that is useless. If we are going to be victorious in life then we need to refuse to be offended. Taking offense hinders God's ultimate plan for our life. We can't go forward, we stay stagnant. Do you know what a body of water looks like that is stagnant and doesn't move? It is nasty, it starts to grow algae and forms green scum all over the top of it. It smells badly too. We want a life that is free to flow Christ through us. We want to move out of that stagnant pond to the living flowing waters that He has for us.

The benefit of God's Word

Make a list of scriptures promises that will help you to see others and situations as God would. This will enable you to look differently at things and not take offense. Copy these scriptures and place in an area that you will see them. Refer to them, especially in times when you want to take offense at someone or something.

And blessed is he who is not offended because of Me.

Matthew 11:6

In return for my love they are my accusers, But I give myself to prayer

Psalm 109:4

But I say to you, love your enemies, bless those who curse you, do good to those who hate you, and pray for those who spitefully use you and persecute you

Matthew 5:44

Declare over your life...

God, your plan for my life is perfect. You have set forth a path of righteousness. You have removed obstacles and allowed freedom for me to flow through it. Help me to see the snares set forth by Satan and to avoid them. Let me walk in truth and love always. Keep me moving forward with my eyes focused on you. Let me not take offense and just let things roll off of me. People and things that come against me do not affect me. I know that you have my life in control. Even when the enemy wants to cause division in my life, I won't take it. Let me show love to others even when they don't deserve it. Remind me that people need you. Christians need you. I need you. Let me be thankful always and rest in your word of truth.

Be ready

Love is the ultimate cure for offenses. It will destroy self-centeredness that thrives on its own self-seeking interest and rights. It will forgive those who disappoint us. Love WILL cover a multitude of sins.

'You shall love the LORD your God with all your heart, with all your soul, and with all your mind.'[a] 38 This is the first and great commandment. 39 And the second is like it: 'You shall love your neighbor as yourself.'

Matthews 22:37-39

Progress continues...

Learning to not take offense at things is something that requires time. It takes time to discipline yourself to do something new. Just as if you were to quit a bad habit or an addiction, taking offense is something that has probably been taught to you from when you were very young. It is not impossible to overcome, it takes awareness and consistency to stop doing it. To ensure progress ask the Lord to help you become aware of situations that you take offense with.

When you are made aware of a situation, write it down. Then work through the steps outlined in this chapter to help you overcome them. Continue doing this until you learn to not take offense at things. This is a continual act of obedience. It requires awareness and time. Habits have been said to take twenty-one days to break. By the time you are finished with this study, if you consistently work at it, you should be on a path freed from offense. Continue coming back to this chapter and write down times that offenses occurred.

> *Trust in the* LORD *with all your heart,*
> *And lean not on your own understanding;*
> *In all your ways acknowledge Him,*
> *And He shall direct your paths.*

> *Proverbs 3:5-6*

OUR NEED TO CONTROL

"Would you let go of the situation and stop trying to fix it, so that I can start doing what it is I need to do?" -God

If your husband would just do as you ask, your children do as they are told, and friends listen to you, then things would go well and life would be perfect, right? Wrong. Hopefully that got a smile from you. We as woman have a huge need to control. God gives great insight into things that only us as woman can see but that doesn't mean that He wants us to be in control of everything.

Control:

- power to influence or direct people's behavior or the course of events

---

CLOUDBURST...MY TESTIMONY

For myself, this was a huge part of my life. I grew up learning to do things my way because it was best. It did not matter what kind of unrest and friction I caused in my home because the bottom line was I knew best! As a new wife, having to adjust to life with a strong willed husband, made the first few years of our marriage a rocky one. He had his way of doing things and I had my way of doing things and, of course, mine were better and right. I was going to fight tooth and nail until I got my way. Our arguments ended in huge fights that would last days, until one of us broke.

Things got worse as I became a Christian and my husband did not. I just thought if I could manipulate this situation and do this thing then he would definitely come to know the Lord. The more I tried to "control" my own little world, the more it made me less and less happy. I thought if we raised the children exactly my way, then they would turn out perfectly. I did not want any type of bad influence to corrupt their lives. It was such a struggle to make things just so "perfect." I would go to sleep many nights crying because I had this lot in life and I couldn't fix it and make it better.

Then it hit me one day while listening to a sermon at church. The pastor was talking about sharing the love of Jesus with others and it wasn't about trying to control the situation and make it perfect so that all would work out, it was about living our lives as Jesus would, being the person that He has called us to be so that He could do the work. He quoted this verse:

Love suffers long and is kind; love does not envy; love does not parade itself, is not puffed up does not behave rudely, does not seek its own, is not provoked, thinks no evil; does not rejoice in iniquity, but rejoices in the truth; [7] bears all things, believes all things, hopes all things, endures all things.

1 Corinthians 13:4-7

That was it. Here I was a new Christian and supposed to be sharing this great life of being a Christian to others, but all I was doing was condemning what they were doing. I wasn't sharing the number one thing that God shares with me, that He loves me. I was not supposed to try and control my life and situations, I was just supposed to love. If I loved, then God could do the work that He needed to do through me towards the people I was struggling with. But I had to first get my life in control and under the obedience of God.

Dynamics of Losing Control and Showing Love

How do we actually break down loving others as God would want us? We take scripture and dissect it line by line and understand what each verse means.

"Love suffers long and is kind"

I wonder how many marriages would be saved today if husbands and wives would make love suffer long, instead of giving up as soon as they "suffered?" Or what if we traded in our meanness and spitefulness for kindness?

"love does not envy; love does not parade itself, is not puffed up;"

If we truly loved, we wouldn't envy what we don't have. We wouldn't walk around, especially to our unsaved spouses or children and act as though we are better than them. We never would have to think that we "knew it all." We would just be content knowing who we are in Christ and where we are in our walk with Him.

"does not behave rudely, does not seek its own, is not provoked, thinks no evil;"

Sometimes we are more prone to treat strangers better than our own loved ones. Things that we would never say to a stranger, we blurt out almost haphazardly to our own. We must think about what words are coming out of our mouths. The Bible says *out of the abundance of the heart, the mouth speaks.* Whatever types of things are in our hearts, proceed out our mouths. When we don't seek our own agenda's, but seek the Lord's, we will walk in love. We can trust and have faith in Him, and won't feel the need to "control" things. We let God do the changing. This is true even if we think we know what God's agenda is for someone else. Evil is the opposite of love. If we are supposed to walk in love and truth, according to the bible there should be no evil in our hearts.

"does not rejoice in iniquity, but rejoices in the truth;"

We as Christians should never rejoice when someone else sins. Seems easy enough right? Sometimes when someone has hurt us or has done wrong to us, deep down we may have a root of bitterness in our hearts and think that "they are going to get theirs!" But we shouldn't be rejoicing in that way, we should be hopeful that those people will turn from their ways. People are lost souls. They have closed their eyes and covered their ears to hearing God's truth. They know not what they do. Jesus tells us to "forgive them." We should pray for our enemies that they would see the light and God's truth.

"bears all things, believes all things, hopes all things, endures all things"

It may appear that the Christian way has to put up with an awful lot--*bearing all, enduring, believing, and hoping.* But if you look to the non Christian they could say that they do the same thing-they bear all their problems, they believe and are hopeful that what they do can change things and make them better. They try and endure things in their life. But that sounds like an awful lot of stress and pressure to put onto one person. Aren't you glad, that we as Christians have someone whom we can believe and hope for while we endure things? How much better is it to know that we have someone whom we can turn to in times of trouble? When we recognize that God is love and that we are to be like Him, we won't have to worry about things of this world. God promises to never leave us nor forsake us. That is a powerful truth.

When we see that the only way that we are supposed to respond and act in this world is in love, we will put down our need for control in life. We are to put our hope and faith in God and hold onto all promises.

WHAT DOES THE BIBLE SAY ABOUT CONTROL?

The Bible is a continuous book of truth on the topic of God being in control when we make Him Lord over our life.

There are many plans in a man's heart,
Nevertheless the LORD's counsel—that will stand.

Proverbs 19:21

And we know that all things work together for good to those who love God, to those who are the called according to His purpose.

Romans 8:28

For I know the thoughts that I think toward you, says the LORD, thoughts of peace and not of evil, to give you a future and a hope.

Jeremiah 29:11

But Jesus looked at them and said to them, "With men this is impossible, but with God all things are possible.

Matthew 19:26

"For My thoughts are not your thoughts,
Nor are your ways My ways," says the LORD.
"For as the heavens are higher than the earth,
So are My ways higher than your ways,
And My thoughts than your thoughts.

Isaiah 55:8-11

Now unto him that is able to do exceeding abundantly above all that we ask or think, according to the power that worketh in us

Ephesians 3:20

Over and over the Bible states that "man's thoughts are not the Lord's." Even in our own infinite brains, we can never comprehend all that God will do. That is why He tells us to put our trust in Him and that NOTHING is impossible. He promises to do EXCEEDINGLY ABUNDANTLY above all that WE could ask or think! That is huge. We have to understand this truth and know that God can do so much better than we can do. When we get out of the way and stop controlling things, God is able to step in and do what He does best----change people from the inside out.

TAKE ACTION: STEPS TO LETTING GO OF CONTROL

1. It 's not about me

2. Life is not a mold

3. Trusting in God and yourself

The need to be in control and critical of things can be an exhausting task to take on. Over time, this can be unhealthy to us physically, emotionally, and spiritually. We will have given up for the one need God made us for---to be dependent upon Him!

Step one: It's not about me.

We need to realize that life and the problems we face are not all about us. Sometimes we put ourselves in this little glass bubble for the world to see. We start thinking and believing that everyone is watching so we start holding ourselves to an unattainable standard. This is especially true with church. How many know others who come to church all spiritual on Sunday but then go home and the rest of their week is falling apart? We need to start living our lives with Christ everyday of the week and for Him and Him alone. We should turn to God, become humble, accept problems and let God fix them. This is by far a better testimony to others of how we should live our life with God in control, not us.

Step two: Life is not a mold

God did not make everyone to fit into a mold. God made each and every person on the earth in His own image and likeness. He made the movers and shakers of this earth. He made the ones that would follow, and the ones that would lead. We are ALL different. You cannot fit you and your family into this perfect mold of what you think life should be. All of us are different. Certain groups may look like they have it all together, but in reality they probably don't. They are human beings. We all fail, we all mess up. But those that live in Christ will rise up and follow His perfect will. When we are unhappy in our own lives, it is much easier to look past the flaws of those put up on a pedestal. People are not perfect, we are not perfect, so stop and re-examine your behavior.

Step three: Trusting in God and in yourself

Most of us will never try and do things out of our comfort zone because of our fear of what will happen. We feel that if we let that one person into our life, then we give up our control. If our children don't behave a certain way, then our reputation is going to be tarnished as a Christian parent. If we just let go of that one string that we control our husband with, then he is going to walk all over us. But we have to know that we are made with so much more depth, strength, flexibility and resilience then we can ever imagine. God's word says that *He never gives us more than we can handle*. That is so very true We can't stay conformed to this little box of life. If we do, we will miss out on great things from God. We have to embrace God and His truths.

The benefit of God's word

Once we grasp the realization that everyone is different in life, then we can start accepting others and situations for who and what they are. This week, take scripture references that will help you grow in your faith towards God. Know that God can be in control of your life, if you let Him. Memorize and repeat them over and over until you feel at peace that God has you and will never leave you.

Come to Me, all you who labor and are heavy laden, and I will give you rest. Take My yoke upon you and learn from Me, for I am gentle and lowly in heart, and you will find rest for your souls.

Matthew 11:28-29

And my God shall supply all your need according to His riches in glory by Christ Jesus.

Philippians 4:19

Peace I leave with you, My peace I give to you; not as the world gives do I give to you. Let not your heart be troubled, neither let it be afraid.

John 14:27

Declare over your life...

God I am giving up my control over to you. I know that you will take charge and lead my life far better than I can. I will not stand in the way to block the purpose for which you have sent me. I will follow through with what you speak to me. I will willingly submit even when I don't understand. I put my complete trust and faith in you and KNOW that you will work ALL things out for my good. I trust you completely.

Be ready...

Letting go and letting God be in control is tough but not impossible. Once you grasp this very important truth, things in life will begin to roll right off of you and into God's hands. I am not an advocator of repeating prayers but I came across this and thought it worthy to share. You may know the Serenity Prayer but most of us do not know the last part of that prayer:

God grant me the serenity
To accept the things I cannot change;
Courage to change the things I can;
And wisdom to know the difference.

Living one day at a time;
Enjoying one moment at a time;
Accepting hardships as the pathway to peace;
Taking, as He did, this sinful world
As it is, not as I would have it;
Trusting that He will make all things right
If I surrender to His Will;
So that I may be reasonably happy in this life
And supremely happy with Him
Forever and ever in the next.

Progress continues...

This week take some time to sit quietly with the Lord to review this truth. Ask Him in what areas do you struggle with giving up control. Write down the areas that He brings to mind. These can include any of the following:

- Finances
- Children's behavior
- Relationship with husband
- How you spend your free time
- Weight issues
- Household clutter
- Lack of time with the Lord

Once you have your list, prayerfully start releasing one by one each area of your life to God. Then take action and have a plan. If one of your areas of control is your weight, then let's break it down. Stop trying to fight how you feel about it Make a list of four things that you can change that would help your weight issue. Examples can include: drinking more water, beginning exercise, cutting out processed foods, eliminating deserts. Now that you have four things, begin with implementing one each week. The first week drink a set amount of water each day. Continue doing this and then the following week add the next item on your list. By the end of the month you will have formed four new habits and will have begun steps to giving up your control over weigh issues.

If you struggle with issues in your marriage, make a list of four things that you can implement within the next month to change in your relationship. Examples can include: making your spouse's favorite meals, including a special treat in their lunch, placing a love note in their car, or making it a point to say, "I love you" each day. Make it be things that go above and beyond what you do normally every day. Plan a date night each week.

That doesn't have to be something that costs, you can just go for a walk together, a long drive, or maybe having a special moment together when all the children go to bed. Whatever the needs, write four things that you can do for each and begin implementing.

Any of the areas that the Lord has brought to mind, prayerfully write out actions that you can do. Begin by making those little changes and then they will become habits. The only way you are going to see something real happen in your life is by doing what God asks of you on your end and then giving the rest over to Him.

And those who know Your name will put their trust in You;
For You, Lord, have not forsaken those who seek You.
Psalm 9:10

Area to work on: _____

Four steps I can do to make a change:

1. _____

2. _____

3. _____

4. _____

Verses for encouragement:

_____

_____

Area to work on:: _____

Four steps I can do to make a change:

1. _____

2. _____

3. _____

4. _____

Verses for encouragement:

_____

_____

Area to work on: ——————————————

Four steps I can do to make a change:

1. _____

2. _____

3. _____

4. _____

Verses for encouragement:

_____

_____

Area to work on:: ——————————————

Four steps I can do to make a change:

1. _____

2. _____

3. _____

4. _____

Verses for encouragement:

_____

_____

DEVALUING OURSELVES IN CHRIST

Be careful of what you say to yourself because your soul is listening.

-author unknown

Can we all admit that we have been guilty of breaking the 10th commandment at least once in our lives?

"You shall not covet"

Many of us have, and may still sit and mull over our life situations and hold a pity party. I can probably share multiple "if only..." or "what if..." scenarios that you have played over and over in your heads. We may think how much easier life would be if we were in a different situation. We look at ourselves and are not happy with the person we have become. We are disappointed in how much we have let our bodies "go" over the years. We are frustrated with the way we have raised our children. We are not happy in our working situation and feel that we may have wasted much of our life doing nothing productive. Our relationship with our husbands may not be going great and we think it may be better to be alone. We have driven ourselves to sit and eat an entire container of chocolate brownie ice cream to make ourselves feel better.

Why is it we think we deserve chocolate brownie ice cream but not all that God has for us?

> **Self worth:**
> - one's worth as a person, as perceived by oneself

God did NOT create us so that we can walk around being defeated. His value on everyone is priceless. No matter what situation you have gone through in life or where you have come from, God loves each and every one of you and has this amazing plan for your life. Even if you think that your situation in life will never get better, I have news for you.....it can! But, you have to want it to get better.

HERE COMES THE DOWNPOUR AKA EXCUSES

Satan devises all kinds of thoughts to make us as women believe that we are not worth enough. You don't have to look very far to see how our society treats girls and women. All over the world they have been degraded and devalued since the beginning of time. We as women and mothers need to know what our value is so that we can equip our daughters and other young women to know what their value is in life. God gives us voices and passion to do things. If He really wanted us to sit around and be dormant He would not have put those feelings inside of us.

Here are some excuses that we make to diminish our value in Christ:

Excuse #1

"My parent's didn't want me, I'm not good enough"

For those that were adopted or may have parents who had left them, did you know that God wanted you? He says in Psalm 27:10, *that even though my father and mother have forsaken me, you the Lord, took me in*. No matter what type of beginning you may have come from, God does not care. He does not care if you came in from the king and queen of a country or from the situation of a rape. He just wanted you here. He knew that He needed you on this earth to complete part of His big plan. He knew that only YOU could fill that part. That is why you are here!

It can be very easy to get down on yourself when you feel that you have no family that you can turn to here on earth. But you have to look at God as the "family" that you need. When we have problems and things to share, go directly to the One who can help you the most. Most people spend an awful lot of time hashing over things with people, when they really need to be going directly to God. He is the one that will help us through our troubles and only He can give us the right answers. Be comforted to know that you make the right choices when you go directly to the One who knows all, your heavenly Father. Don't base your life on where you started from, base it on where God is taking you.

Excuse #2

"God has forgotten me"

What if you haven't felt Him in a long time? What if things seem to be going wrong over and over again? Do you believe that the Lord could forget you?

> Can a woman forget her nursing child,
> And not have compassion on the son of her womb?
> Surely they may forget,
> Yet I will not forget you

Isaiah 49:15

Think of what it is like to be nursing a baby. That baby is in complete need of you and you alone. No one else can do. When that baby is in another part of the home and begins to start whimpering, instantly your body reacts and starts to produce milk for it. Even if when you hold that baby and the cries have escalated, your body produces more substance to the point that it is overflowing and too much. But as soon as that baby latches on and realizes that they have what they need, then they can rest with contentment.

This is a direct parallel for us. God does not forget us. When we start whimpering, God hears us. He is there, ready to take care of us, but we don't go to Him right away. We usually wait, until we are so done and beyond ourselves and then we will finally say, "Okay God, thank you." He faithfully takes care of us. Never believe that God has forgotten you, because He hasn't. We ourselves have forgotten the One to turn to.

Excuse #3

"Well this is the way that God made me."

News flash.......God DID NOT make you to be defeated, down trodden, or depressed in any way, shape, or form. We can't use the excuse that we are just depressed, or have anger issues, or anxiety issues and can't amount to anything. That is a lie from the devil himself. God made each and every one with a perfect plan and purpose.

You may look at others and see them going and doing but it is not because they have better personality skills than you do. It is because they are DOING. God gives everyone exactly what they need to do things in life. We are all different. We all have different skill sets, different personalities, and different ways that we operate. If we didn't, our entire world would be a very plain land. Everyone would be the same. We would have no excitement, nothing to look forward to, life would just be a cycle of blah. We need the quirky, crazy ones to liven up the place a bit, but we also need the more serious, quiet ones to bring that balance into play when it is needed. Don't ever look at yourself and be upset with the way that you are. Discover who you are so that you can bring that special touch into our world.

Excuse# 4

"Everyone has it better than I do, I am just not as skilled as they are"

God has made each and every one of us with different gifting and skills. When we all pull together and do what it is God wants us to do, then and only then, can our world live in a perfected harmony. It is not that anyone else is more "perfected" than you are it is that they have tuned into that perfection and went with it. You have that perfection in you. Stop letting the negativity drown out what God has in you. We all have some gifting. Find what you are best at doing and hone in on those skills. Ask God what you can do with what He has given to you. Learn how to operate in the realm that God intended for you. I guarantee that you will be blessed.

Excuse #5

"I can't do anything because it will usurp my authority over my husband"

This is one that I have experienced in my own life and I believe it holds back many women because they are afraid to step out into what God has for them. I myself got into this rut of believing that I was not as valued, as my husband was in Christ. I believed in submitting to my husband, keeping quiet, and feeling insecure in who I was. I felt like I could never speak up, that God could never use me, and that I was to remain quiet and not cause any conflict. I came to experience that submission was more of a control and a bondage by my own doing.

Before we continue, I am not against submission. But I think that what it means to submit has gotten eschewed over time. Women have believed countless lies based on tradition and not the Word of God.

God never intended for women to be less than men. The garden incident is always blamed on the woman. But if you read God's Word it says that sin came in through one MAN. Not a woman. God had given the responsibility to the MAN to tend the garden, to watch over it and to guard it. When God was calling out to Adam and Eve after they had eaten of the tree, He asked Adam why he was hiding. Now God knows all but He was looking for Adam to take responsibility. He asked him why he was ashamed. Adam's response was that the woman had made him eat from the tree. He was casting blame. When God had asked Eve, she confessed her sin to Him. She didn't cast blame, she repented. Whose job was it to tend the garden, to keep out the serpents from corrupting it?

He gave man the woman to be his help meet. Being a help meet does not mean to be beaten or torn down, or to be taken advantage of. Woman was not taken out of his foot, so that she could be under him, she was taken out of the side to be next to him. The Bible said that she COMPLETED him. She made him whole. We were made to be part of each other, not for woman to be separate or to be less. Without us, they are not complete. They NEED us.

It is very evident in our day that we have many men that do not accept their responsibility to tend and rule the garden as God commanded Adam. We have many single moms and many married moms who take on the role as Mother and Father. Men want to have the authority to rule and run their garden, but none of them want to take the responsibility to guard it and tend it. Some men just want to go to work at their jobs and then come home and sit. They expect the woman to take care of the house, to clean it, to provide meals for it, to get the groceries, to tend the children, run the family here and there, to take care of finances, to worry about how to make those finances work, and some of these woman have employment out of the home that they are responsible for as well. But they are still expected to "fulfill their place in the home."

We want our men to be strong leaders. I have a strong husband that is easy going, he lets me have my way in many things. But when he puts his foot down, his foot is down. The fact that I can respect that is important. We have a good relationship. It's been a work in progress, but we are working and that is key.

God wants to use each and every one of us women, but we have to know how to use that gifting and then STILL be a devoted wife at home. Just because God may have given you a ministry, does not mean that we need to be "more than a man." We don't need to think that we are higher because God gave this to us. We just have to know that God gave gifting and we are to do with it as He asks. We don't have to do that with a rebellious attitude. We should be working towards being one and showing love with our husbands.

Okay, sounds wonderful, but what if my husband isn't doing as he should? What if he doesn't lead our family? What if he expects me to do everything? What if he isn't living a life for Christ at all? My answer: PRAYER. Pray that our men rise up to become leaders in the home. We need to ask God for discernment to know where and what we are to do. We don't want to let our "gifting" step over and interfere with what God is going to do in our husbands. Communication and openness is an important key. We don't need to behave in such a way that is usurping authority over our husbands.

It begins with our hearts and our attitudes. God can bless you and work things out with a heathen of a husband just as much as a God fearing man but we need to have our hearts right with God. Continually ask the Lord for a cleansing of your heart so that your intentions are not deceiving and your motives are pure. The important key is that WE do as God wants US to do as wives and women. When we do as God asks of us we can confidently rest with our decisions and where He has us in life.

Who may ascend into the hill of the LORD?
Or who may stand in His holy place?
He who has clean hands and a pure heart,
Who has not lifted up his soul to an idol,
Nor sworn deceitfully.
He shall receive blessing from the LORD,
And righteousness from the God of his salvation.

Psalm 24:3-5

WHAT DOES THE BIBLE SAY ABOUT OUR SELF-WORTH?

For You formed my inward parts;
You covered me in my mother's womb.
I will praise You, for I am fearfully and wonderfully made;
Marvelous are Your works,
And that my soul knows very well.
My frame was not hidden from You,
When I was made in secret,
And skillfully wrought in the lowest parts of the earth.
Your eyes saw my substance, being yet unformed.
And in Your book they all were written,
The days fashioned for me,
When as yet there were none of them.

Psalm 139:13-16

We are wonderfully made! All of the days of our lives were written in God's book BEFORE we were even born. This means that God knows the plan for our lives. That means that he HAS a plan. That plan does not include us sitting around wasting it on self pity and sadness.

Then God said, "Let Us make man in Our image, according to Our likeness;

Genesis 1:26

Did God just say that He wants us to be made in HIS image? We all were made in the image of God. Sin then entered the world and it became corrupted. We still are made in the image of God, but sin has made us flawed. This is the reason we have need for a Savior so that we can be put back to the perfect acceptable place with God.

and that you put on the new man which was created according to God, in true righteousness and holiness.

After we accept Christ as our Savior, we then put on our new man and become a new creation. In 1 Thessalonians 5:23 it says that we are made up of three things--spirit, soul, and body. Our bodies still stay the same, when we accept Jesus we won't get a new one until later on, make sure to take care of it. All of the parts that make up our unique personality: our mind, will, and emotions, are what make up our soul and that remains the same. But, our spirit changes. Our spirit becomes one with God. It becomes one of righteousness and holiness. As we read God's Word and get closer in our relationship with Him, our soul will also begin to be changed. We will become more like God and all His wonderful attributes of love and goodness.

God values us so much that He has written an entire book devoted for our benefit. It has many words of affirmation, plans to prosper us, and encouragement to see us excel in life. It is truth. Truth for you and me, to know where we stand in our walk with God and who we are as a person in Christ Jesus.

NAVIGATING THE STORM

Now that we know where we stand in Christ Jesus according to God's Word, what are some practical things we can do in everyday life to help see our true worth in Him?

Stop comparing ourselves to other woman

When we compare ourselves to other's we are coveting what they have. The Bible tells us not to do this. We can't look at someone else, who is in a completely different life than ours and think that we can have that. We need to be content at the season we are in and know that God is molding us towards our "perfected" life. No one on the earth is the exact same. We are all made with different talents, skills, and gifting. When we start coveting and trying to be like others, we are going against God's ultimate plan for us. Stop and start seeking God for what He wants in your life.

Don't let the words of other's define who you are

I remember an important truth that my Mom always told me, "When other's treat you meanly it is because they are unhappy in their own lives." This is a huge lesson for everyone. Know that people are hurting. People are angry and are lost. Even well meaning Christians, still have heart issues to work on. Just because someone says something hurtful or unkind, it isn't usually about us. It is normally something that they are insecure with. Someone who is secure in their life has no need to go around saying nasty remarks to others. Stop listening to others and start listening from God. Don't value your life on how others treat you. If you are doing what it is God wants you to do, then you have to be content with that. You leave the rest up to Him.

If your husband, friend, or family member is constantly coming at you with negativity, you have to do what the Bible says. The Bible tells us to love our enemies and treat them with kindness.

Do not be overcome by evil, but overcome evil with good.

Romans 12:21

You have to do everything that God wants YOU to do and then you can step back and not worry about anything. You did your part and now God can do His.

Remember that media is only a half-truth and never shows the entire picture of things.

How many of us have favorite television shows that depict perfect looking families? We have blogs that we follow that seem to be written by great women having zero flaws. The social media world can make moms to appear perfected or flawed for that matter. But those are only half-truths. If we were to really see into the lives of others, we would be able to see that people have most of the same issues that we have. Even though it looks perfected on the outside, inside there may be more issues going on. Sometimes it is how we react and deal with those issues that make them big or small. No one has a perfect life, no matter how great it appears. But we can have fullness of life by living our lives for Jesus.

Start looking at all of your strengths and stop honing in on your weaknesses

This is the only way to start seeing your value in Christ. If you are continually looking at all of your flaws or all of the wrong things in your life, then you are never going to see the goodness in it. Stop focusing on what you don't have and start focusing on what you do have. Don't look at how far you have to go, look at how far you have come. If God is putting something on your heart, then He will make it work out. You don't need to force the issue, it will happen. Continue seeking God daily. When your best friend is Jesus, what do you have to worry? Your best friend has your back always.

Take Action: Steps to positive self-worth

1. Believe

2. Stop

3. Speak

Step 1: Believe

The first step to realizing your worth in Christ is to believe in yourself and to be content with where God has you. When I first became a Christian, it took me a long time to realize my worth in Christ Jesus. I couldn't believe that He would really take care of me and my needs. I worried about things constantly. Then these verses became a constant reminder to my days:

Look at the birds of the air, for they neither sow nor reap nor gather into barns; yet your heavenly Father feeds them. Are you not of more value than they? Which of you by worrying can add one cubit to his stature?

"So why do you worry about clothing? Consider the lilies of the field, how they grow: they neither toil nor spin; and yet I say to you that even Solomon in all his glory was not arrayed like one of these. Now if God so clothes the grass of the field, which today is, and tomorrow is thrown into the oven, will He not much more clothe you, O you of little faith?

"Therefore do not worry, saying, 'What shall we eat?' or 'What shall we drink?' or 'What shall we wear?' For after all these things the Gentiles seek. For your heavenly Father knows that you need all these things. But seek first the kingdom of God and His righteousness, and all these things shall be added to you. Therefore do not worry about tomorrow, for tomorrow will worry about its own things. Sufficient for the day is its own trouble.

Matthew 6:26-34

If God took care of the birds of the air and the lilies of the field, how much more does He care for a human being made after His image? I remember taking a bird nest that we had found outside and I put in it a decorative sparrow. I placed this in my kitchen as a constant visual reminder that God would take care of me. When life started feeling a little uncertain, I would look at my bird and be reminded that God would take care of me.

"Are not five sparrows sold for two copper coins? And not one of them is forgotten before God. But the very hairs of your head are all numbered. Do not fear therefore; you are of more value than many sparrows.

Luke 12:6-7

Know who you are and where you stand with Christ.

Step 2: Stop

If we are ever going to move forward in our lives then we need to stop listening to others and their negativity towards life. If you have friends who are constantly being negative, you might think about stepping away from that relationship for a while. Surround yourself with people who will build you up and do not tear you down. If that person is a spouse, you can't obviously step down, but have scripture memorized and quote it over and over again in your head. The next time they come around with negative remarks, you will have God's Word to fill your mind with good things. You won't need to receive any of the negativity and it will keep your mind focused on God and all His goodness. When someone throws something at you that is against God, search the scriptures and find what God has to say about it. Quote it over and over, until it is implanted into your heart.

Step 3: Speak

The best way to fight off Satan and His attacks is to speak the Word of God to him and tell him to leave. When things go bad, get out your Bible reference list and start quoting scripture. Repeat it over and over until that negativity is gone. Know that as soon as you are on the right path to living victoriously in Christ, Satan is immediately right there to steal, kill, and destroy. He knows that if he can put doubt in your mind, then he has won. You have to doubt the doubt. Keep your mind, will, and emotions focused on God. Speak out the words until they become routine in your life.

THE BENEFIT OF GOD'S WORD

The only way to bring about a change in how you view yourself is if you get your soul to agree with what the Word of God says. How that is done, is by applying the scriptures. You need to memorize God's word, applying it daily to your life, and believe it. The more this becomes natural, the more that your soul---your mind, will, and emotions will be changed. Copy down scripture references that help you see your value in Christ. Here are some examples:

For I know the thoughts that I think toward you, says the LORD, thoughts of peace and not of evil, to give you a future and a hope.

Jeremiah 29:11

And we know that all things work together for good to those who love God, to those who are the called according to His purpose.

Romans 8:28

I have been crucified with Christ; it is no longer I who live, but Christ lives in me; and the life which I now live in the flesh I live by faith in the Son of God, who loved me and gave Himself for me.

Galatians 2:20

If we confess our sins, He is faithful and just to forgive us our sins and to cleanse us from all unrighteousness.

1 John 1:9

Declare over your life...

I am seeking God's will for MY life and I will work towards becoming the woman He intends for me to be. I will not accept negativity from others, I will only listen to what the Word of God says about me. His word says: I am loved, cherished, of value, and made in His image. I know that He has a plan for me. He will never leave me nor forsake me, and I can give him complete control over my life and rest in that assurance. It does not matter what my current situation is in life, God has a far better ending for my life than what is going on now. His ways are higher than my ways and only He knows what is best for me. I will wait with confident expectancy and will do all that He asks of me so that I can get to the perfected place. I willingly expect good things and am excited that the Lord allows me the ability to be used by Him.

Be ready...

Remember that when you are going to have a breakthrough in your life that does not make the devil happy. He prefers to keep you in your current state of mind. He does not want you to be made aware of all that God has for you. His plan is to keep you bounded in lies. When things start to go wrong in life know that it isn't about what is really going on in the physical realm, it is happening in the spiritual realm. The Word of God says:

For we do not wrestle against flesh and blood, but against principalities, against powers, against the rulers of the darkness of this age, against spiritual hosts of wickedness in the heavenly places.

Ephesians 6:12

When things start to go wrong here, know that in the spiritual realm, a battle is being fought. Satan's angels know that God's angels are being awakened and coming to cover in your life. They are going to start stirring things up to make you doubt what you just learned. You have to stay strong, positive, and know that you have nothing to fear. Stand on the Word of God and be confident:

Therefore submit to God. Resist the devil and he will flee from you

James 4:7

The Word of God says that the devil must flee from you. Once he knows that he is no longer a threat to you, he will flee. It is our job to continue doing what God's Word says:

Stand fast therefore in the liberty by which Christ has made us free, and do not be entangled again with a yoke of bondage.

Galatians 5:1

Even when you think that you know it and are firm on it, be careful because he prowls around looking for a weak spot to enter. There may be some area in your life that you allow him authority. It is our job to be on watch.

Be sober, be vigilant; because your adversary the devil walks about like a roaring lion, seeking whom he may devour. Resist him, steadfast in the faith, knowing that the same sufferings are experienced by your brotherhood in the world.

1 Peter 5:8-9

We already know the end of the story......that God's side wins. We don't have to worry about Satan prevailing, because we know that those who love the Lord and follow Him, have nothing to fear. We already won. We don't need to make any battle bigger than what we want it to be. Stop running around the mountains in your life and start dissolving them as God's Word says:

So Jesus answered and said to them, "Have faith in God. For assuredly, I say to you, whoever says to this mountain, 'Be removed and be cast into the sea,' and does not doubt in his heart, but believes that those things he says will be done, he will have whatever he says. Therefore I say to you, whatever things you ask when you pray, believe that you receive them, and you will have them.

Mark 11:22-24

If we have no doubt in our hearts, then the mountains will be removed. But if we doubt any part of the Word of God, then we can't really believe that things will work out. We will then keep running around and around our mountains. Stop being a mountain climber and start being a dissolver!

Progress continues...

This week's lesson is about getting our soul-- our mind, will, and emotions, lined up with what the Word of God says about us.

If we can get our souls to believe what God says, then we can have true victory in our lives.

The only way that we can get this to happen is by overcoming the doubts that we do have. I want you to begin to focus on the positives in your life instead of the negatives. Each day, write down five positive things about yourself and then look up verses to solidify what you believe. Meditate on them and memorize the scriptures. Once you begin to do this, it will start to become part of you and you will no longer look at your life like the world has taught you. Your mind will be transformed and you will begin to see yourself as Christ sees you.

Here are some examples:

I am far from oppression, and fear does not come near me

In righteousness you shall be established;
You shall be far from oppression, for you shall not fear;
And from terror, for it shall not come near you.

Isaiah 54:14

I have the mind of Christ

For "who has known the mind of the LORD that he may instruct Him?" But we have the mind of Christ.

1 Corinthians 2:16

I have the peace of God that passes all understanding

and the peace of God, which surpasses all understanding, will guard your hearts and minds through Christ Jesus.

Philippians 4:7

I have no lack for my God supplies all of my need according to His riches in glory by Christ Jesus

And my God shall supply all your need according to His riches in glory by Christ Jesus.

Philippians 4:19

I can do all things through Christ Jesus

I can do all things through Christ¹ who strengthens me.

Philippians 4:13

I am more than a conqueror through Him who loves me

Yet in all these things we are more than conquerors through Him who loved us.

Romans 8:37

I am the head and not the tail; I am above only and not beneath

And the LORD will make you the head and not the tail; you shall be above only, and not be beneath

Deuteronomy 28:13

I am the light of the world

You are the light of the world. A city that is set on a hill cannot be hidden.

Matthew 5:14

I am forgiven of all my sins and washed in the Blood

In Him we have redemption through His blood, the forgiveness of sins, according to the riches of His grace

Ephesians 1:7

I am redeemed from the curse of sin, sickness, and poverty

Christ has redeemed us from the curse of the law, having become a curse for us (for it is written, "Cursed is everyone who hangs on a tree")

Galatians 3:13

I am firmly rooted, built up, established in my faith and overflowing with gratitude

...rooted and built up in Him and established in the faith, as you have been taught, abounding in it with thanksgiving.

Colossians 2:7

I am healed by the stripes of Jesus

And by His stripes we are healed.

Isaiah 53:5

My mind is clear and sound because God has not given fear to me. I have love and power in my life.

For God has not given us a spirit of fear, but of power and of love and of a sound mind

2 Timothy 1:7

I do not live alone in life but with Christ inside of me guiding me in my ways.

I have been crucified with Christ; it is no longer I who live, but Christ lives in me; and the life which I now live in the flesh I live by faith in the Son of God, who loved me and gave Himself for me.

Galatians 2:20

FINDING CONTENTMENT AMONG THE STORM

Finding your faith and trusting in God is the only way to achieve true contentment in life. This will lead to peace and happiness that will rule over you. When you can be content where you are at, and with what God is doing in your life, then nothing else will bother you. As long as you are doing your part, God will do His part.

If we want God to work through and in our lives daily, then we need to do the same. We should turn to the Word of God and make it a priority each and every day. Stop using the excuses that you don't have time. We all have the same 24 hours each day. If you were to prayerfully ask God where you can find an extra 20 minutes, He will be faithful to show you. I am a Mom and know how hard it is to find an extra few minutes each day. When I earnestly sought the Lord for finding more time, I was amazed at when I just started spending that time in the morning, how much better my days and weeks went. I was able to get the same amount of work done and still have time to spend in God's word. Finding more time to spend with God is about recognizing our priorities and which ones we need to change so that we can work on our relationship with Him.

God wants to bless you and show you where you need to be going in life. Most start out strong with the Lord and then are real quick to jump out of it when the storms of life start rolling in. Our natural inclination is to try and run and hide, but if we turn to God and allow Him to fix things we will be amazed by the results. We need to wait patiently for God to work them out.

Isn't it nice that we can hand over our problems to God and not have to worry about them? Most of us do not. We want to keep holding onto our baggage and drag it around with us everywhere we go. It weighs us down and does not allow us to jump into new opportunities or new places because it is heavy and too hard to handle. Letting go is a freeing experience. It says to your problems, " I don't have to deal with you anymore, I am moving on to greater things in my life."

Think of a storm rolling in, you can see it coming from a distance. In our natural state, we can't do anything about it, it still comes. If we are rooted and grounded in the Word of God then when the rain starts falling it won't affect us. We are able to put up our umbrellas---the Word of God and be protected and safe from the storms. The storms will continue to come and rain will fall, but those that are under the protection of God Almighty will rest assured knowing that God has them.

For as the rain comes down, and the snow from heaven,
And do not return there,
But water the earth,
And make it bring forth and bud,
That it may give seed to the sower
And bread to the eater,
So shall My word be that goes forth from My mouth;
It shall not return to Me void,
But it shall accomplish what I please,
And it shall prosper in the thing for which I sent it.

"For you shall go out with joy,
And be led out with peace;
The mountains and the hills
Shall break forth into singing before you,
And all the trees of the field shall clap their hands.
Instead of the thorn shall come up the cypress tree,
And instead of the brier shall come up the myrtle tree;
And it shall be to the LORD for a name,
For an everlasting sign that shall not be cut off."

Isaiah 55:10-13

Authors note:

I pray you have been blessed by doing this study. If you have been working diligently throughout this book, I would love to hear the results that you have had. I want to hear the testimonies of how God has set you free from your bondages. If you still struggle, go back and apply the steps as outlined in the chapters. Keep meditating on the Word, speaking it over and over. Even if you don't feel freed from it, still continue to speak it! The results will come!

Send me an email at plainandnotsoplain@gmail.com

Be blessed,

Amy